D1706313

NIMALS

Cats

by Hollie Endres

BELLWETHER MEDIA · MINNEAPOLIS, MN

Note to Librarians, Teachers, and Parents:

Blastoff! Readers are carefully developed by literacy experts and combine standards-based content with developmentally-appropriate text.

Level 1 provides the most support through repetition of high-frequency words, light text, predictable sentence patterns, and strong visual support.

Level 2 offers early readers a bit more challenge through varied simple sentences, increased text load, and less repetition of high frequency words.

Level 3 advances early-fluent readers toward fluency through increased text and concept load, less reliance on visuals, longer sentences, and more literary language.

Level 4 builds reading stamina by providing more text per page, increased use of punctuation, greater variation in sentence patterns, and increasingly challenging vocabulary.

Level 5 encourages children to move from "learning to read" to "reading to learn" by providing even more text, varied writing styles, and less familiar topics.

Whichever book is right for your reader, Blastoff! Readers are the perfect books to build confidence and encourage a love of reading that will last a lifetime!

This edition first published in 2008 by Bellwether Media.

No part of this publication may be reproduced in whole or in part without written permission of the publisher. For information regarding permission, write to Bellwether Media Inc., Attention: Permissions Department, Post Office Box 1C, Minnetonka, MN 55345-9998.

Library of Congress Cataloging-in-Publication Data
Endres, Hollie J.
  Cats / by Hollie J. Endres.
    p. cm. — (Blastoff! readers. Farm animals)
Summary: "A basic introduction to cats and how they live on the farm. Simple text and full color photographs. Developed by literacy experts for students in kindergarten through third grade"—Provided by publisher.
  Includes bibliographical references and index.
  ISBN-13: 978-1-60014-111-9 (hardcover : alk. paper)
  ISBN-10: 1-60014-111-0 (hardcover : alk. paper)
  1. Cats—Juvenile literature. I. Title.

SF445.7.E53 2008
636.8—dc22   2007007461

Contents

Some cats live
on farms. Farm
cats may live
in the barn
or the house.

Cats have soft fur.
Cats clean their fur
with their tongue.

Cats have
whiskers.
Cats use whiskers
to feel things
around them.

Cats **hunt** mice
on the farm.
These cats
watch for mice.

Cats have sharp **claws**. They use their claws to catch mice.

Cats can leap
through the air
when they hunt.

Cats like to
hunt at night.
They see well
in the dark.

This cat got
a mouse!

19

Cats like to sleep
during the day.
They rest in
the warm sun.

Glossary

claws—sharp, curved toenails on an animal

hunt—to follow an animal in order to kill and eat it

whiskers—thick, strong hairs on an animal's face used to feel things

To Learn More

AT THE LIBRARY

Ganeri, Anita. *Cats*. Chicago, Ill.: Heinemann, 2003.

Santoro, Scott. *Farm-Fresh Cats*. New York: HarperCollins, 2006.

Schuh, Mari C. *Cats on the Farm*. Mankato, Minn.: Capstone Press, 2003.

ON THE WEB

Learning more about farm animals is as easy as 1, 2, 3.

1. Go to www.factsurfer.com

2. Enter "farm animals" into search box.

3. Click the "Surf" button and you will see a list of related web sites.

With factsurfer.com, finding more information is just a click away.

Index

The photographs in this book are reproduced through the courtesy of: Stephen Orsillo, front cover; Shawn Hine, p. 5; JC, p. 7; Sergey Ilin, p. 9; Antonio Jorge Nunes, p. 11; Blickwinkel/Alamy, p. 13; Sami Sarkis/Getty Images, p. 15; Kobi Israel/Alamy, p. 17; Andrey Stratilatov, p. 19; coko, p. 21.